With its open vistas and vast skies, Wicken Fen is a window onto a lost East Anglian landscape. It is a living reminder of the wetlands that the fens once were – both land and water at the same time. Hidden within this extraordinary terrain lies a wealth of wildlife, flora and fauna. In fact, over 9,000 species have been recorded here.

Deep peat bogs, laid down millennia ago in the flooded lowlands of East Anglia, created the fens and at Wicken they still remain. Although this land has been shaped by centuries of human activity, it has never been drained. How we look after Wicken today echoes traditional ways used since the fifteenth century and gives us a glimpse of how fen dwellers lived off this land in the past, season by season. It was naturalists who saved the Fen as it faced pressures in the nineteenth century; today they have been replaced by volunteers, enthusiasts and scientific researchers, people who still retain the pioneering spirit of those Victorian conservationists. Known as the 'birth place of ecology', Wicken is still at the forefront of nature conservation.

Wicken Fen was the first nature reserve to be owned by the National Trust; indeed it was one of its first properties, celebrating its centenary in May 1999. Over 100 years on, Wicken is now home to the Trust's largest lowland landscape restoration project. Known as the Wicken Fen Vision, the overall scheme has ambitions far beyond its current boundaries; the plan is to expand the size of the reserve dramatically, providing a buffer zone for the core wetland and re-establishing habitats that had been lost. Carried out on this scale, we can be sure of creating a sustainable future for many fenland species.

'My personal feeling about Wicken is a complicated one: a mixture of enjoyment of fenland plants and animals (both aesthetically and scientifically), glimpsing the past and sensing the passage of time, while all the time enjoying the great open fen landscape under its vast skies. Of course I have little vignettes of special memory. For example watching swallow-tails emerging from their pupae, looking at Adventurers' Fen in 1940 knowing it was soon to be destroyed and more recently the enjoyment of being part of a very special endeavour to understand Wicken and conserve it. To me Wicken is the first English Nature Reserve, a very special wetland and the most famous fen.'

Dr Norman Moore, former
Chair of the Wicken Committee

The Fens

The area known as the fens is bordered by the counties of Lincolnshire, Norfolk, Suffolk and Cambridgeshire. It was formed when sea levels rose at the end of the last Ice Age, about 12,000 years ago. As the ice moved northwards, drainage of the fenland basin deteriorated, and the area flooded. The remains of dead plants did not decay in this waterlogged ground, but accumulated as peat. The forest that had covered the region still surfaces occasionally in the form of ancient trees referred to as 'bog oaks'.

Human settlement was limited to the 'isles' of clay, places such as Ely and Wicken village, and the drier uplands on the margins of the marshland, for example the villages of Burwell and Swaffham Prior, south-east of Wicken. The wet fens, however, were important to local people as they provided food (fish and wildfowl), fuel (peat and sedge), building materials (peat and clay for bricks, sedge and reed for roofing), and animal feed and bedding.

The push to drain

External pressure to drain the wetlands, to control flooding and improve their agricultural potential, has been strong over the centuries.

The Romans attempted drainage, building the Car Dyke between Lincoln and Cambridge to channel water away from rivers that crossed the fens. They also constructed some of the waterways known locally as lodes, including Reach Lode, though many of these date from later centuries. However, after 200 years, Roman cultivation of the area declined as sea levels rose again.

The Normans built banks: the 'Roman Bank', a 60-mile long earthwork around the Wash, which was reconstructed and lasted for 500 years, protecting more than 404,500 hectares (a million acres) of land. Powerful monasteries such as at Peterborough and Ramsey were instrumental in local land reclamation but their fisheries and waterfowl remained important to them. By the fourteenth century, the fens were one of the wealthiest parts of rural England, because of the unique wet landscape and the variety of products it provided.

Left Professor Albert Seward poses with an excavated bog oak in the fens, while on a 1935 field trip with the University of Cambridge's Fenland Research Committee. The whole tree has been preserved in the rich peat soil

A winter view to the south-west, across Baker's and Adventurers' Fens, towards Burwell Fen. The bare black peat fields, and those covered with polythene, of the agricultural land beyond contrast with the vegetation of the nature reserve

After the Dissolution of the Monasteries
in the reign of Henry VIII, church land was
redistributed, often to colleges and to courtiers
living elsewhere. Maintaining embankments was
not a priority for them, resulting in disastrous
floods in 1603. The greatest advance in draining
the fens began after this. James I vowed to
prevent the area from laying to waste and came
up with coordinated plans for drainage.

The 4th Earl of Bedford and other land
speculators, then called 'merchant adventurers',
paid for this drainage, bringing in a Dutchman,
Cornelius Vermuyden, to oversee the plans.
Large-scale schemes undertaken in the 1630s,
including rerouting the River Ouse and digging
the Bedford River, were partially successful, but
were interrupted by the Civil War. Work on an
elaborate system of drains and river diversions
resumed in 1649; prisoners were used to dig the
New Bedford River, and create new washes to
take floodwater. The scheme was unpopular with
locals as it infringed property rights and offered
no compensation. Fen dwellers were made
responsible for maintaining water courses which
they had not asked for and which damaged the
natural ecology as well as their livelihoods. As a
result, there were popular uprisings, resistance
and sabotage, by the so-called 'Fen Tigers'.
The villagers of Wicken, armed with pitchforks,
had succeeded in 1637 in seeing off the king's
messengers who had come to claim 237 hectares
(585 acres) for the adventurers, and as a result
saved their fen from drainage.

In a major oversight, Vermuyden had not taken
account of the effect of peat shrinkage which
caused land levels to become lower and lower.
Water now had to be pumped up, instead of
draining it into rivers by gravity – and it still does.
Local drainage boards, many of them set up
in the 1700s, are still responsible for keeping
farmland drained, while the pumping of water
is funded by landowners.

Today, flooding of the drained fens can
mostly be contained, but there is still a danger
of inundation when certain weather and tidal
conditions prevail, and the pumps simply cannot
cope. The disastrous floods of 1947 caused
widespread damage.

Wicken Fen: The First 100 Years as a Nature Reserve

The National Trust was just three years old when Herbert Goss, a distinguished entomologist, suggested that it should consider saving Wicken Fen, 'the haunt of much wildlife'.

On 1 May 1899, the Trust bought 0.8 hectares (two acres) of fenland from Goss's fellow entomologist, J. C. Moberley. More sections were bought or donated steadily over the years. In 1901 the Hon. Charles Rothschild, founder of the Society for the Promotion of Nature Reserves and an influential figure in the early days of nature conservation, donated parts of St Edmund's Fen and Adventurers' Fen – the latter named after those early venture capitalists who invested in land drainage.

George Henry Verrall (1848–1911) was one of the most important benefactors to Wicken Fen. He worked in horseracing and moved from Lewes in Sussex to Newmarket in 1878. He became the town's Conservative MP in 1910. His fascination with insects, flies in particular, led him to purchase several tracts of Wicken Fen, to preserve it. He bequeathed 97 hectares (239 acres) to the National Trust – parts of Sedge Fen, St Edmund's Fen, and what is now called Verrall's Fen.

Scientists, watchers, keepers and wardens

Amateur naturalists have always been present at Wicken Fen, at first even managing the Fen for the National Trust and providing the necessary specialist knowledge. The Local Committee for Management was first appointed in 1911, to manage the Fen 'to the best interests of the naturalists and others and to the best financial advantage consistent with such interests'. The National Trust only had representation on the committee from 1926.

From 1914, the Committee employed a 'Watcher' of the Fen, G. W. Barnes, upgraded to the role of 'Keeper' in 1925. Keeper Barnes was joined by his sons, Henry, William and Wilfred, who tried so far as possible to continue the traditional methods and patterns of sedge cutting and peat digging that had occurred for centuries. The Barnes family worked at Wicken Fen for most of the century; Wilfred retired in 1987.

Opposite left 19th century collectors came to the fens looking for beetles and moths; here they pose in front of harvested sedge

Above The Barnes brothers, Wilfred (left) and Henry (right) with Lieutenant Colonel Charles Mitchell take a break from the 1967 sedge harvest

Above Wicken villagers, such as Albert Houghton (right), supplemented their income by guiding visitors to the best collecting spots. He is here with an 'Eddystone Lighthouse' moth trap, in 1894

In 1936, a new secretary of the Committee, William Thorpe, drew up the first management plan for Wicken. As a result, additional finance was forthcoming from the National Trust to employ four extra labourers to clear bush. However, they only lasted a fortnight; heavy rain ended this first attempt to restore open habitat.

Routine work suffered during the Second World War as only Henry Barnes and his father remained on the Fen throughout. The War Office requisitioned Adventurers' Fen, and had it redrained for food production. Thankfully William Thorpe did manage to prevent the draining of Sedge Fen, as well as the use of the wider area as a practice bombing range. The National Trust regained control of

Adventurers' Fen after the war, and the programme of wildlife conservation began once more. The Mere was dug and opened officially by Peter Scott, founder of the World Wide Fund for Nature (WWF) and the Wildfowl and Wetlands Trust, in 1955. The Tower Hide was built soon after, to provide visitors with a view of the new landscape on Adventurers' Fen.

Lieutenant Colonel Charles Mitchell was appointed as the first full-time Warden of the Fen in 1961. He concentrated on reinstating systematic cropping regimes and on raising funds to purchase the necessary power-operated tools. He drew up a new management plan to stem deterioration of the Fen, and brought in volunteer work parties on a large scale to remove scrub. In 1969, the William Thorpe Building was opened as a laboratory and lecture room; in 1996, it was refurbished and now functions as the Visitor Centre, with offices for staff.

Wicken Fen has been important in developing many research techniques, such as 'pollen analysis', which traces the history of an area's vegetation by examining pollen and plant remains preserved in peat. A close working relationship between the relevant faculties at Cambridge University, other universities and the Fen staff is maintained. Many research projects continue at Wicken Fen, everything from evaluating eco-systems services, whereby the all-round benefits, such as recreational and cultural value, carbon sequestration and water purification, provided by an eco-system are accounted for, to fieldwork which monitors the evolutionary 'arms race' between cuckoos and reed warblers.

Left Sedge harvesting
through much of the 20th
century looked very similar
to the work of the previous
400 years

Habitats of the Old Fen

Wicken Fen now consists of a number of distinct areas – the old Sedge Fen, which remains undrained, Adventurers' Fen, and land which has been more recently acquired. The latter is in various stages of reversion from agriculture to land managed for wildlife.

Sedge fields

Sedge hath its home
oftest in fen
groweth in water
woundeth grimly
blood draweth
from any man
that maketh any
grasp at it.
(Saxon Runic poem)

Great fen saw-sedge *(Cladium mariscus)* is what
defines the Sedge Fen. Earliest written records
of sedge harvesting at Wicken date back to 1419.
The crop was so valuable to local people that they
resisted seventeenth-century drainage plans for
the Fen. The sedge is still cut by the rangers, both
preserving a rare habitat and keeping alive an
historic practice.

Sedge is harvested after three or four years'
growth, so as not to weaken it and let other
grasses become dominant. This infrequent
cutting allows a wide variety of other water-
dependent plants and insects to flourish in the
sedge fields. These include rarities such as milk
parsley and marsh pea.

Left Reeds fringe the
ditches which criss-cross
the old Sedge Fen

Above Lepidopterists (moth and butterfly collectors) on Sedge Fen, 1899. Mature willow trees now found on Sedge Fen Drove originated as poles they stuck in the ground, covered with sugar solution, to attract moths to catch

While the value of the sedge saved Wicken Fen from earlier drainage, the beetles and moths proved to be its saving grace at the end of the nineteenth century. Just as the market for sedge and peat collapsed, the Victorian interest in natural history, and in creating collections of specimens, reached its peak. With most of the surrounding fenland drained, Sedge Fen became a mecca for entomologists and botanists, many of them associated with the University of Cambridge. The number of moth traps on the Fen at night prompted one commentator to compare the sight to city streetlights. These Victorian naturalists proved ready buyers for the land; they could see that unless they preserved their valuable hunting ground, the old Sedge Fen too would be drained for agriculture. And from 1899 the National Trust took on the mantle from these individuals.

Sedge, however, is vulnerable to the process of succession. Only the repeated cropping since the fifteenth century had prevented its natural replacement by trees but for various reasons, scrub or 'carr' (wooded wetland) encroached on the open Fen during much of the twentieth century. In 1900, only seven percent of Sedge Fen and Verrall's Fen was bushes and trees. By 1997, carr represented 76 percent of these areas while sedge only remained on ten percent.

Despite owning a large area of the Fen, the Trust and management committee were able to employ only Keeper Barnes and his sons, compared to the 50 or so villagers who formerly worked the land. They simply could not cut as much each year. Merging many small plots, previously worked individually, into larger fields also discouraged diversity.

Early attempts to secure good breeding grounds for Montagu harriers, by simply leaving Verrall's Fen alone, had the opposite effect as the open fen was steadily taken over by carr.

The Fen also began to dry out, threatening the classic fen habitat. A sluice and pump installed at Upware in the 1940s stopped winter flooding; summer levels in Wicken Lode became lower than before, as more water was used for crops in surrounding farmland.

From the 1960s, scrub removal became a major part of restoration work, only possible through volunteer labour. Crew members of the training ship HMS Ganges were among the first organised work parties, not only clearing the Fen, but also erecting the 'Ganges Hut' in 1965 – basic dormitory-style accommodation for volunteers. In 2001 it was refurbished as a classroom for visiting schools.

Scrub removal was accelerated as part of Wicken Fen's Centenary Project, in 1999, with the help of a Heritage Lottery Grant. The grant paid for a workforce, equipped with heavy machinery, for five years. A visit to Sedge Fen now gives more of an idea of what a visitor in 1900 would have experienced, with uninterrupted open fen vistas.

Look out for

- Marsh pea (1), flowering in June and July on the edges of the sedge fields, a rare plant that is relatively easily seen here
- Field strips of sedge (2) at different stages of growth, from young green shoots, to tall brown sharp-edged plants when three or four years old
- Milk parsley (3), flowering in July, in the sedge fields
- Marsh harriers (4) in summer, and hen harriers in winter, quartering the fields
- Rangers and volunteers cutting sedge in July and August

Fen meadows

1

Many of the open areas of the Fen are species-rich wet meadow communities dominated by grasses, known as 'litter'. Cut at Wicken from the late nineteenth century for use as hay, and used for covering the floors of Newmarket racing stables, litter became a significant crop after the slump in the sedge market. Its typical plant species were not abundant before then as the management of the Fen was geared towards sedge production.

The litter fields are valuable for the wide range of invertebrates supported by the diversity of plants. There are in fact two types of litter vegetation, one dominated by purple moor-grass and the other by small-reed species. The areas with purple moor-grass are less widespread and mainly at the western edge of Sedge Fen near Drainer's Dyke; it only thrives where scrub or carr has not previously invaded.

The litter fields are divided into small areas, and a complicated pattern of cutting is in place to promote as much diversity as possible. Some plots are cut annually, some biennially, and some two years in three. There is also seasonal variation in the cutting. This allows for different species to be favoured in seed setting and dispersal, and in germination and seedling growth conditions. These same conditions prevailed in the seventeenth century when the Fen was owned and worked by numerous people, creating a diversity of flora and fauna. Our management of the litter meadows today is designed to replicate this pattern.

Look out for

- Hen harriers, returning to roost on the Fen in the evening, and barn owls (1), hunting low for small rodents, in the winter
- Yellow loosestrife (2), flowering in July and August
- Devil's bit scabious (3), in flower from June to October
- Purple loosestrife, flowering from June to August
- Snipe (5), which nest in the Fen meadows
- Marsh thistle, spiney and up to two metres tall, flowering from June to October

Ecology's oldest experiment

Harry Godwin first visited Wicken Fen in 1921. He was studying Botany at Clare College, Cambridge and cycled out one day as a member of the university Ecology Club. During the 1920s he started a landmark experiment that is still running today in the north-west corner of Sedge Fen by establishing what are today called the 'Godwin Plots' (4). These show what happens to plant communities under different cutting regimes. Neighbouring plots are cut every four, three or two years, annually or never at all – the last plot is now covered with scrub. This experiment demonstrates that sedge fields can easily be converted to litter by cutting them every two or three years.

At the time, the idea that management alone could affect plant communities was radical – now it forms the basis of nature reserve management. Harry Godwin was knighted in 1970.

Droves

The grass paths across the Fen are known as droves (1). They may well follow the routes of tracks dating from as far back as 1666. Sedge Fen Drove is certainly at least 300 years old. Together with Gardiner's Drove it provides access across the Sedge Fen.

The droves are between five and ten metres wide, the central part mown for ease of access for visitors and Fen staff. The wide borders on either side are cut in the autumn to provide a short, species-rich sward. The obvious disturbance caused by human feet and machinery means that there are more short-growing plants than in the meadows. Plants such as spike-rushes and marsh arrowgrass grow here; jointed rush occurs on the trampled central strip of the droves while blunt-flowered rush grows in the side strips. There are places on some of the droves that are almost always wet – ideal for early-sprouting sweet grasses, as well as rare soldier flies and craneflies.

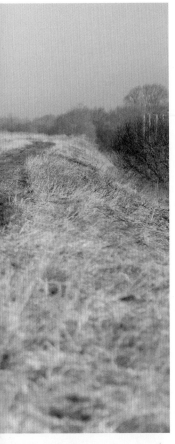

Look out for

- Common comfrey (2), abundant on the Fen, and favoured by bumblebees
- Yellow rattle (3), flowering in July. Listen to it rattle later in the year, traditionally when it is time to harvest
- Early marsh orchid and southern marsh orchid (4), flowering in June
- Common lizard (5), sunbathing on the Boardwalk
- Silverweed (6), a flat-growing member of the rose family, ideally suited to heavy traffic
- Ragged-robin (7), flowering from May to July

Lodes, ditches and drains

Wicken Lode, which divides the reserve, is one of a number of ancient man-made waterways in the South Cambridgeshire fens. Mostly constructed in the Middle Ages (although Reach Lode may be Roman in origin) the lodes were designed to control the winter water levels of fenland pasture.

Their later use, though, was mostly for transportation. Running from fen-edge villages on the chalk upland to the River Cam, they provided navigable water access across the fens both to the sea and to major markets such as Cambridge. Monk's Lode from Newmarket meets Wicken Lode; Burwell Lode forms the eastern boundary of Adventurers' Fen, running from Burwell to the Cam at Upware.

The lodes carry drainage water from the ditches and drains that criss-cross the fens.

Abov e A fen boat heavily laden with sedge makes its way along Wicken Lode

While the water in Wicken Lode is slightly below the land surface of Sedge Fen, it is above the level of the drained Adventurers' Fen (1). All the other lodes in the area are several metres above the drained farmland, which is protected by waterproof banks built up to prevent flooding of the fields.

The water in Monk's Lode and Wicken Lode is of very high quality, supporting a rich diversity of flora and fauna.

A network of ditches, or dykes, and smaller drains dissects Sedge Fen. The oldest of these is probably Drainer's Dyke, dug in the seventeenth century. Running from Spinney Bank down to Wicken Lode it cuts between Sedge Fen and Verrall's Fen.

As well as being drainage channels, these ditches provided access to individual plots of sedge and peat diggings for the villagers. They also acted as boundary markers. As the pattern of ownership changed and the cutting of sedge declined, they fell into disuse; many became choked by vegetation and dried up. Evidence of them remains as damp depressions in the ground.

Each stage in the life of a ditch or dyke favours particular species. Some dragonflies prefer open water, while reed warblers favour reed-fringed ditch edges for nest building. The water rail likes a ditch where only a narrow shallow channel of water remains. While the ditches are cleared regularly, this work is not done across all of them simultaneously. Different habitats from one ditch to the next are maintained in this way. Some of the rotations for 'slubbing', as ditch clearance is called, are on cycles of up to 12 years.

In the lodes, look out for

- Mute swans (2), their large nests are unmistakable
- Reed warblers (3), nesting and sometimes acting as unwitting parents to cuckoo chicks
- Water lilies, water mint, arrowhead, with different shaped leaves above and below the water, and hornwort, which is completely submerged
- Kingfishers (5)
- Fish, many different species, including bitterling which lay their eggs in freshwater mussels

In the ditches and drains, look out for

- Grass snakes swimming in hot weather
- Many species of dragonfly and damselfly, including emerald damselfly (July to September), red-eyed damselfly (May to August), southern hawker dragonfly (July to September) and ruddy darter (July and August)
- Variable damselfly (4), again nationally notable, but a common species on the Fen (June and July)
- Stoneworts, in the dyke alongside Gardiner's Drove, favoured by snails
- Greater bladderwort, Wicken's only carnivorous plant, each one eating up to a quarter of a million invertebrates annually

Carr

Carr is wet, or even waterlogged, scrub woodland (4). **Its spread at Wicken is relatively new.**

Common species are alder buckthorn, common buckthorn, willows, guelder rose and hawthorn. These bushes and small trees grow up to 15 feet. While the ground is too wet to support large old trees, in some areas birches, and even ash, oak and alder, do grow up through the carr. Given time and with no human intervention, these trees would develop into woodland. Although too many trees on the reserve are detrimental to the classic fen habitat, Cambridgeshire has relatively few woods and so they are a valuable environment for some animals and plants.

The characteristic plants of sedge and litter communities do not survive in the thick carr areas, although some other plants do well. These are notably marsh fern, mosses and liverworts, and fen nettle. The variety of ferns is increasing, with more woodland ferns appearing; similarly the list of mosses and lichens is now much longer than in the mid-twentieth century. Birds and insects are not abundant in areas of old-established carr, but are more frequently found on the edges of new carr.

The wooded area near to the Brickpits, where the gault clay rises close to the surface, has existed since the early nineteenth century. There are apple trees near the sites where brick workers' cottages once stood.

Alder buckthorn (3) was not recorded at Wicken Fen until 1861 but by the end of the nineteenth century it was 'abundant', the seeds spread by birds which were fond of its berries. Bushes became established with reduced sedge cutting, growing best on the ridges of peat workings, rather than in the furrows which flooded in winter. Once established, impenetrable thickets soon develop, with the crowns forming a closed canopy.

It was coppiced in the Second World War as its charcoal was ideal for making bomb fuses. While it seemed at the time to be a way to clear bushes, the stumps remained and in fact rapidly generated new growth. It did, however, provide income (£10 per ton), and this was useful in the argument against using Adventurers' Fen as a bombing practice range.

Look – and listen – out for

- Flocks of fieldfares (1), feeding on alder buckthorn berries, September onwards
- Brimstone butterflies (2), both alder and common buckthorn are its food plants
- Guelder rose (5), actually a type of honeysuckle, white flowers in June, bright red berry clusters through the winter
- Woodpeckers (6) tapping
- Woodcock, grasshopper warblers, woodpeckers and owls

Adventurers' Fen

1

The area south of Wicken Lode differs from Sedge Fen, having been partially drained in the past. With wet grassland, water, and reed beds, it offers a patchwork of habitats attractive to many birds.

The 'merchant adventurers', speculators who financed drainage schemes in return for the land, claimed the area south of Wicken Lode, towards Burwell Lode, in 1636. Theirs was a poor investment though; drainage was not achieved until 1840. The land was briefly given over to agriculture, and then large-scale turf digging. By the end of the nineteenth century, several windpumps were needed to keep the turf-pits drained. When the demand for peat collapsed, they fell into disuse, and water, reeds and wildfowl reclaimed the low-lying land.

The National Trust acquired much of this area in the first part of the twentieth century. Charles Rothschild donated 12 hectares (30 acres) to the National Trust in 1901, and the rest of the area now covered by the Mere and reed beds was acquired between 1912 and 1939 from Bill Norman, farmer, turf (peat) and coal merchant in Wicken.

During the Second World War Adventurers' Fen was once more cleared and drained for food production, as part of the Dig for Victory Campaign. This is documented in a book *Farm on the Fen* by Alan Bloom, and a 1941 film shows extraordinary footage of massive bog oaks being exploded. After the war, however, the land was returned to the National Trust, and was allowed to revert to wet meadows and reed beds.

The Mere was dug between 1952 and 1955, specifically to encourage wildfowl. It is home to a diverse range of birds in the winter months. The National Trust bought Baker's Fen in 1993,

adjacent to the land around the Mere. It is part of the wider Adventurers' Fen, and has been restored from arable to wet pasture. Wintering, migrant and breeding birds are all now using the area.

The reed beds

The reed beds on Adventurers' Fen are a valuable habitat for many insects and birds. Inland reed beds will become increasingly important as coastal areas come under threat from rising sea levels.

While reed has been harvested at Wicken in the past this is no longer a viable practice. The annual cutting required to produce good thatching reed is detrimental to such species as the reed leopard moth, for instance, which has a two-year maturation inside the reed stem before it appears. The reed beds used to be cut on a four-year cycle to benefit wildlife; current management is much less intensive and is only done to prevent scrub encroachment. Newer areas of the reserve are likely to develop into reed bed over time.

Below Groups of roe deer (2) can often be seen on Adventurers' and Burwell Fens

Look out for

- Grazing herds of konik ponies (1) and Highland cattle
- Lapwing (3), on the wet grasslands all year, but large flocks in winter
- Wigeon, teal, shoveler, on the Mere, large numbers in winter (4)
- Bittern, and bearded tits in the reeds around the Mere, most months
- Cormorants, on the island trees in the Mere, all year
- Marsh harriers, during the summer months

Ebbing and Flowing Biodiversity

Wicken Fen survives today because Victorian naturalists recognised its importance as a refuge for rare wetland plants and animals in a dry and intensively farmed landscape. Due to their efforts and those of many naturalists since, the Fen has one of the longest species lists of any reserve in Britain, over 9,000 in all. The records list is far from complete – some groups have hardly been studied – but it includes more than 2,000 species of dipteran flies; 1,000 species of beetle and 1,000 of moths; 212 species of spiders; and nearly 300 species of vascular plants. While some of these are no longer present at Wicken there are new sightings recently added that would surprise a nineteenth-century observer.

Some species have become more vulnerable, even disappearing, for a number of reasons including lack of water, the changing acidity of the soil and the loss of open habitat. Past collecting by enthusiasts hasn't helped either, so while the Fen was saved, individual highly sought-after species were still at risk. In a few cases, such as the twin spot longhorn beetle (*Oberea oculata*) and the crucifix ground beetle (*Panagaeus cruxmajor*) it is unclear whether or not a small hidden population is still at the Fen.

Lost to Wicken Fen

• The swallowtail butterfly (1), the iconic species of Wicken, sadly now extinct here, despite several controlled reintroductions. Its caterpillar's sole food plant, the milk parsley, has performed poorly because of the past drying-out of the fen. Work to improve the sedge fields should increase and safeguard the milk parsley population – and in the long term make Wicken a viable site for the swallowtail once more. Currently, all native swallowtails are found in the Norfolk Broads, where their favoured habitat is buffered by miles of similar land

• The common hawker dragonfly (2), one of several species associated with the acidic conditions generated by turf-digging

• White-clawed crayfish (3)

• The fen orchid (4) last recorded here in 1945. Its decline was the result of both over-enthusiastic specimen collecting, and the end of peat digging which provided suitable 'open' habitat

• Various moths, including reed tussock, marsh dagger, the many-lined and gypsy moth (5)

Rare species still at Wicken Fen

• The fen violet (*Viola persicifolia*) (1) is only present in the wild at three sites in England. It was recorded by C. C. Babington in his *Flora of Cambridgeshire* of 1860 as one of the species that 'most abound' at Wicken. By the end of the nineteenth century it was only rarely seen, and by the 1920s it was considered extinct in the Fen. The earlier abundance noticed by Babington was probably the result of peat digging, which had all but stopped. In 1980, a single seedling was spotted in soil samples that had been taken from beneath scrub on the Fen. In 1982, a large flowering population was discovered on Verrall's Fen – this population flourished through the 1990s. It then disappeared, only to be rediscovered in 2014, a few years after grazing koniks were brought in. The fen violet seems to flourish in recently cleared areas, when the peat is laid bare. After a few seasons, other plants will spread into the area, and the violets are eliminated once more. However, it seems the violet's long-lived seeds are what ensures its long-term survival even if it is crowded out by more dominant plants in the short term. With grazing now on Verrall's Fen, plus occasional scrub management, producing the right conditions, the fen violet has shown its resilience.

• Otters (2) returned to Wicken Fen in 1999 after an absence of 60 years.

• Bitterns (3) were breeding on Adventurers' Fen between Wicken and Burwell up until 1937,

the reed habitat in this area, before it was drained, being ideal for them. As the Wicken Fen reed beds became more established in the second half of the twentieth century, bitterns over-wintered for many years. As the area under conservation management has grown, bitterns are now present and breeding again on the reed beds.

• Water voles (4) were spotted again in 2006, and are now often seen in the ditches on Sedge Fen and Baker's Fen.

Some newcomers

The changing landscape of the Fen has benefited other species, that would not previously have been comfortable here. Drier conditions, more trees and bushes, and changing acidity have brought the following species, all new to the reserve since 1950. Some species are increasing their range generally as a result of climate change.

• Woodcock
• Emperor dragonfly and black-tailed skimmer
• Muntjac and Chinese water deer
• Brown argus butterfly
• Crickets such as Roesel's bush-cricket and the long-winged conehead
• Lady-fern, male-fern, narrow buckler-fern
• Hairy dragonfly (5), a recent return to Wicken Fen as a result of improved ditch management, nationally a notable species (May and June)

The Fenman's Cottage

'The Lode', now Lode Lane, was once a thriving hamlet with a separate identity to the rest of Wicken village, the livelihoods of its inhabitants being closely tied to the fen.

They relied upon the traditional harvesting of sedge, reed, litter and buckthorn (which was used in making gunpowder), digging peat and clay, and the shooting and trapping of wildfowl, eels and fish. They also controlled the movement of these fen goods, and of incoming goods for the village, via the lode and river network.

The cottage at 5 Lode Lane is a rare survival of local vernacular building. Like many smaller houses, it has been altered and extended to accommodate more people. The oldest part, the thatched end, dates from around 1700. Originally it was a simple layout, divided only by the central brick stack with an open hearth. The pantiled end of the cottage was probably added in the late eighteenth century to provide room for a second family. Its roof was originally thatch, but was replaced (and raised to create a sleeping loft) after being destroyed in a storm at the beginning of the last century. The pantry was originally a small dairy, accessed from the outside, rather than an integral part of the house. The lean-to kitchen is a Victorian addition built as a 'backhouse' with a copper for washing, and a bread oven.

In 1825 James Butcher, labourer and turf cutter, moved into the newer part of the cottage with his wife Caroline Howlett; her family, recorded in Wicken records as far back as 1636, owned the cottage. James was the first of four generations of Butchers to live here. By his death in 1886 he owned the older portion of the building; in 1900 his son George bought the newer part for £5, one of several properties he owned on the lane.

After a period away, farming in Upware, George returned in 1924 with his widowed daughter-in-law Alice, and disabled grandson Reggie. He joined the two parts of the cottage into one residence. George died in 1936, but Alice and Reggie remained until her death in 1972.

Reggie was unable to work on the fen, but made a living by selling household items, hatching eggs, making fretwork items and issuing fishing licences. Reggie's bedroom at the rear of the cottage was built on for him due to his disability – otherwise he would have slept in the loft.

Below *Sedge-cutting in Wicken Fen, Cambridgeshire, Early Morning* by Robert Walker Macbeth, 1878

The National Trust bought the cottage in 1974, Reggie having moved out on doctor's orders to live somewhere drier – he just moved to the top of the lane. The cottage was restored between 1988 and 1990 using traditional methods and local materials. It is furnished as it might have been in the 1930s.

The materials used are the same as those in earlier fen 'hovels', which were traditionally built on wooden piles driven into the peat, or on mattresses of reeds and osiers, and with willow and sedge roofs, and walls of 'clay-bats' lined with sun-dried peat-blocks. They were flexible structures suited to the marshy ground on which they stood.

Using fenland materials in house building

Peat blocks are sun-dried, and used like bricks, protected from the rain by a coat of lime plaster. Gault clay, which underlies the Fen, is dug for making bricks, floor pamments (tiles) and roofing pantiles. It is also used to make daub, plaster and limewash. (There are flooded brick pits and the remains of a brick kiln on the reserve.) Reed, harvested from the Fen, is tied in bundles to use as infill in the walls, for the thatched roof, and as a base for ceiling plasters.

Sedge, also cut from the Fen, is added to daub and plaster, and is also used for thatching, often just the roof ridges as it bends more easily than reed, but also for full roofs like the shed or boat house.

Locally quarried lime is essential in traditional mortars and plasters, daub and limewash.

Working in the Fens

Above Boating in the fens is now mostly for leisure, rather than a necessary means of accessing fields and transporting goods

The fenman's calendar was dictated by the cycle of the year, dependent on water levels, bird movements and local harvesting times. Most 'labourers' combined wildfowling, mole catching, the cutting of sedge, osier and peat, and fishing to make ends meet. In the winter, speed skating races were held with winners supplementing their family's food with prizes of meat and cheese.

As the pre-drainage fens were large areas of marsh, the lodes, those man-made waterways of the fens, became vital links between settlements for transporting goods around the area. Wicken Lode connects Wicken with other fen-edge villages like Burwell and Reach, as well as larger markets like Cambridge and Ely. Traditional fen boats were between 20 and 25 feet long and about six feet wide; fen lighters – a type of barge – were between 40 and 50 feet long and were of shallow draft to be able to work in low water levels. They were unique cargo-carrying boats made of wood, flat-bottomed and rounded at bow and stern; their design harked back to the Vikings. Lighters were mostly pulled by horse or donkey, or used a single square sail, and were often worked in gangs. A horse-pulled gang of three lighters transported sedge and turf along Wicken Lode until the 1940s. Warehouses filled with this valuable cargo used to stand at the end of the Lode.

Brick-making in the fens

Evidence of the local brick industry can be seen on the eastern edge of Sedge Fen. Here, there is a complex of brickpits, where the peat gives way to clay on the fen edge. Before the brick workings were developed, the area was listed in the 1842 Tithe Award as part grass, part arable and part woodland – quite distinct from the fen habitat. In 1869 one John Owers, a brick-maker from nearby Soham, bought a plot. By 1880 his brickyard was in full operation, with a kiln and a windpump to keep the pits dry. The yard was still operational in 1894, but by 1901 had fallen into disuse. The remains of the kiln can still be seen. The brickpits have long since filled with water and are now an important open area of freshwater for wildlife. The sites of brickworkers' cottages, on Sedge Fen Drove as it enters Little Breed Fen, are revealed by what once grew in the gardens – snowdrops, for instance, and fruit trees. Many of the Victorian gentlemen collectors stayed in these cottages, known to them as 'Catch-'em-all', when visiting the Sedge Fen for moth hunting.

Wind power

The wooden windpump is a reminder of the old industry of the fens: peat digging. Before the advent of steam and diesel pumping engines, wind power was the major force enabling drainage of the turf pits (peat diggings) and fields.

Originally located near Harrison's Drove on the edge of Adventurers' Fen, this windpump was one of six used to drain turf pits in the latter part of the nineteenth century. It fell into disrepair when turf digging stopped, but was rescued from dilapidation, dismantled, moved and restored in 1956. The windpump at Wicken Fen is now the only one, out of thousands that used to exist, in working order still to be seen in the fens. It is now set up to pump water from the ditch onto the land, but can flood the visitor route when run for demonstration!

Wicken Fen after the Centenary

To celebrate the Fen's centenary year in 1999, the National Trust embarked on a five-year project to restore Wicken Fen to its wetland glory, and secure its future. Additionally, the National Trust launched an exciting and ambitious plan for the next 100 years, the Wicken Fen Vision. This aims to create a truly landscape-scale nature reserve of 20 square miles (53 square kilometres).

One of the main parts of the Centenary Project was the restoration of Sedge Fen and Verrall's Fen. For reasons of historical continuity and the preservation of rare habitat, one of the main aims had to be, once and for all, the clearance of scrub, and the restoration of large areas of continually harvested fen. Five centuries of sedge-cutting is

a remarkable record for sustained management for one crop, and the continuity of one vegetation type.

Litter and sedge fields have been reinstated in the centre of Sedge Fen, and are once again cut in distinctive strips. The water supply to the centre of the Fen was improved by reopening some long-lost ditches. A team of rangers removed 54 hectares (133 acres) of scrub from Verrall's Fen. While the rest of Sedge Fen is still cut, konik ponies were introduced to graze on Verrall's Fen in 2001; their presence prevents the scrub taking hold again. They were joined by highland cattle in 2012 (1).

In 2011, the Environment Agency funded a new windpump (2), to provide clean alkaline ground water to Sedge Fen. This will reverse the drying out of the Fen, pumping in the winter months to lift water from Monk's Lode into the Sedge Fen ditches.

No longer just the preserve of specialist naturalists and collectors, Wicken Fen's twenty-first century facilities need to be suitable for a wide range of people. A larger classroom space was developed, and a new Tower Hide was built to give views over Verrall's Fen. One of the most important factors in providing easy all-year access, the Boardwalk, was renewed and rerouted, using recycled plastic; its original hardwood boards had decayed in the wet peat, and required much day-to-day maintenance. Other developments to improve the visitor experience at the Fen since 2000 include opening the café, offering cycle hire and running boat trips along Wicken Lode.

Wicken Fen – the Vision

Surrounded by intensive agriculture, the old core of the Fen remains vulnerable. Any pressure on its plants or animals, for example extreme weather or fire, can have severe consequences for them, but it is impossible to safeguard every species. The best way to protect Sedge Fen is to enlarge the area managed for conservation and so create a buffer zone. Large-scale habitat restoration, developing in a natural fashion by stopping drainage and allowing large herbivores to graze, will encourage landscape-scale wildlife to colonise. Birds such as cranes, short-eared owls and avocets are already coming back to Burwell Fen. The fenland landscape will become more like that in Eric Ennion's classic book *Adventurers' Fen*, (1942) which describes the area prior to the drainage undertaken in the Second World War.

Grazing for conservation

That Sedge Fen has never been grazed sets Wicken apart from all other surviving fenland fragments in this country and contributes to the distinctiveness of Wicken's flora and fauna. Over the wider area, however, low-density grazing is now necessary, to keep the landscape open and free of scrub. Family groups of hardy highland cattle and koniks range freely over a wide area, staying out all year with minimal human interference. Koniks and highlands were chosen for their hardiness and ability to cope in wetland conditions, as well as having temperaments suited to the presence of people.

Why expand the reserve?

- Protection for vulnerable species by creating new larger areas of habitat. Landscape-scale is a more sustainable model than attempting to manage small, isolated nature reserves.
- Conservation will allow preservation of deep peat layers in the Fen whereas exposure through continued ploughing and arable farming releases more carbon into the atmosphere.
- Compensation for the inevitable loss of wetland near the coast as a result of rising sea levels, for example Wicken's inland reedbeds provide an alternative as coastal areas become brackish.
- Creation of a landscape in which people can enjoy wildlife, walking, cycling and green space.

Wrapped up well, winter birdwatchers congregate at sunset to catch a glimpse of hen harriers coming in to roost

The horses and cattle prefer to eat different plants, and being able to wander at will it is they, rather than us, who will determine what the landscape will look like in the future. The horses, for example, favour soft, sweet grasses, and create a mosaic of short-cropped grass mixed with areas of taller vegetation; cattle cannot graze as selectively, and leave a more tussocky appearance on the ground as they pull at the vegetation.

We don't worm our animals – but we do study their poo! Over 2,600 viable seeds belonging to 18 plant families germinated from horse dung samples collected at Wicken Fen during the course of a year!

The Wicken Fen Vision gives us a fantastic opportunity to introduce more natural methods of large-scale habitat restoration and management, and to be more relaxed about the outcome. We have no fixed end point goal, apart from obtaining, in the long term, a large area of land more in tune with natural processes for both wildlife and people.

Wicken Fen offers a classic undrained fen, full of rare species. It is recognised with every designation for wildlife conservation, is one of the most important wetlands in Europe, and is an iconic ecological asset with a fascinating history. It is also home, now, to one of the most ambitious landscape-scale conservation projects in lowland Britain and at the forefront of twenty-first century ecology.

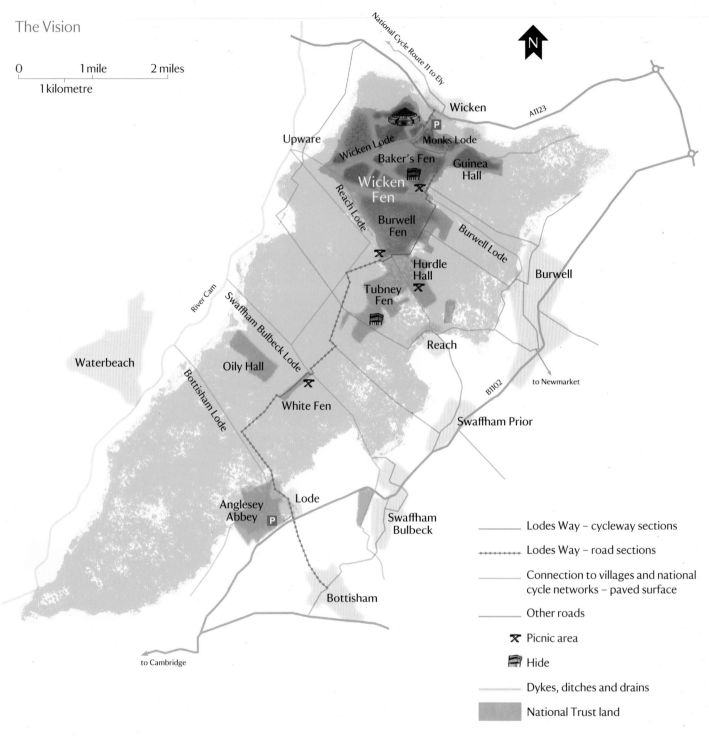

The Vision

0 ... 1 mile ... 2 miles

1 kilometre

National Cycle Route 11 to Ely

N

Wicken

A1123

Upware

Wicken Lode

Monks Lode

Baker's Fen

Guinea Hall

Wicken Fen

Reach Lode

Burwell Fen

Burwell Lode

Burwell

Hurdle Hall

Tubney Fen

River Cam

Swaffham Bulbeck Lode

Reach

Waterbeach

Oily Hall

B1102

to Newmarket

Bottisham Lode

White Fen

Swaffham Prior

Anglesey Abbey

Lode

Swaffham Bulbeck

to Cambridge

Bottisham

Lodes Way – cycleway sections

Lodes Way – road sections

Connection to villages and national cycle networks – paved surface

Other roads

Picnic area

Hide

Dykes, ditches and drains

National Trust land